SHADOWS

SHADOWS

A Collection of Broken Dreams and Heartaches

Aren K. Manahan

iUniverse, Inc.
Bloomington

SHADOWS
A COLLECTION OF BROKEN DREAMS AND HEARTACHES

Copyright © 2012 by Aren K. Manahan.

All rights reserved. No part of this book may be used or reproduced by any means, graphic, electronic, or mechanical, including photocopying, recording, taping or by any information storage retrieval system without the written permission of the publisher except in the case of brief quotations embodied in critical articles and reviews.

iUniverse books may be ordered through booksellers or by contacting:

iUniverse
1663 Liberty Drive
Bloomington, IN 47403
www.iuniverse.com
1-800-Authors (1-800-288-4677)

Because of the dynamic nature of the Internet, any web addresses or links contained in this book may have changed since publication and may no longer be valid. The views expressed in this work are solely those of the author and do not necessarily reflect the views of the publisher, and the publisher hereby disclaims any responsibility for them.

Any people depicted in stock imagery provided by Thinkstock are models, and such images are being used for illustrative purposes only.
Certain stock imagery © Thinkstock.

ISBN: 978-1-4759-6351-9 (sc)
ISBN: 978-1-4759-6352-6 (hc)
ISBN: 978-1-4759-6353-3 (ebk)

Library of Congress Control Number: 2012921992

Printed in the United States of America

iUniverse rev. date: 12/13/2012

For my sister, Sunny.
Thank you for bringing in rays of light in
my darkest hour.

Contents

SECTION I 1

Where Is My Winter Wonderland? 3
Darkness 7
Abandoned 11
Dream 15
Kiss of Death 19
Aurora 23
Love's Ghost 33
Emptiness 37
Sorrow 41
One Wish 45
Lake of Shadows 49
Starlight 55
The Last Waltz 59
Memory 63
Fading 67
Lost 71

SECTION II 75

Angel 77
A Cry for Help 81
Gone Too Soon 85
Regrets 89
Lady in Blue 93

Letting Go 103
Falling 107
Spring Fling 111
Thief in the Night 115
Fall from Grace 119
Destiny 123
Perseverance 127
A Glimpse of Light 131
Roots 135
A Point in Time 139
Farewell 143

Introduction

Basic raw emotions—they can lift you up as if you were floating on a cloud and can just as easily let you spiral down. It is perplexing, when you think about it, how we can allow our emotions to dictate our lives. At the happiest times, people tend to allow everyone in their lives, basking in all of the joy. On the flip side, when saddened, people tend to shy away and retreat to solitude. Some do it to keep others at bay; others do it to protect themselves from getting hurt further.

Heartache of any type has a way of intruding on one's life, regardless of the source, the pain will always hurt. Its how we choose to deal with it that makes the difference. Sometimes, when it becomes too overwhelming, some lash out—or even worse, they start to hide their true feelings, putting on a façade.

The focus of this book will be heartache—not only how it affects people, but also how they chose to deal with it. This book is titled *Shadows*, as that is what these pieces are: a once-glorious feeling turned ill, with only the memory remaining to haunt us.

This collection of short stories and free form poetry is inspired by society as I have seen it and been able to relate to it. Though the stories I have heard or witnessed may not be the same, I was able to relate to the pain, and I know others can too. Something or someone has caused the heart to tear a little bit more. Some of us have been able to pull out of this state of disarray, but others need to go through a few more heartaches before taking control of the pain.

The characters in *Shadows* feel a great deal of pain, mostly because they are alone, dwell in misery, and refuse to allow anyone else in. They are too scared to let down their guard and perhaps even a little ashamed of their feelings. The pain then becomes a secret that is swept under the rug, allowing it to haunt them. The characters are comforted with these feelings, and they make a choice of how they will work through their issues.

To further emphasize the characters' emotional states of being, some of the stories are accompanied by images. They are not meant to be an addition to the book, but an enhancement to the text to provide more insight to the story.

Shadows, highlights the hurt that we all feel at times. As stated earlier, some are able to cope with the pain, and for others, it destroys them. *Shadows* will emphasize the fact that not everyone is fortunate enough to have a happy ending. We have all had shadows pass through us at one point in time, and it is time we confront and let them go.

Section I

Lock the doors; close the windows. In the dark I shall hide. Let nothing in, for winter shall conceal my light and let me slumber in my disarray.

Where Is My Winter Wonderland?

Where Is My Winter Wonderland?

Songs of joy and hope,
Yet loneliness is the only emotion that exists.
A season full of warmth and love and yet unable to melt a heart turned cold.

Why was I so stubborn?
Why couldn't I put my pride aside?
Everything had to be my way; perfection is all I looked for.
All the while you loved my imperfections.

You left, and so did the Yuletide cheer.
The rock I placed upon your hand is now only a lump of coal you left behind.

No chestnuts roasting on an open fire,
No sleigh bells ringing,
No treetops glistening.

Slowly breaking with each passing day, the only gift I look for is a mended heart.
Where is my winter wonderland?

Darkness

Darkness

An empty vessel: a mere shell labeled as a body. Loneliness and agony
are the only feelings that dwell within.
        He can still hear the cries of his helpless mother,
          Still feel the pain of a fist plummeting to his face,
Unable to endure any more blows, the bones break.
        The lost child was too small to fight back.
          A growing boy, he vows revenge. Becoming a man,
          his sorrow and pain turn only into hate.
There is no passage for the light to enter, only utter darkness;
Rather than resisting, he embraces it with open arms.

He seeks comfort in a drink to ease the hardship he has seen.
It is an unquenchable thirst, bringing the shell one step closer
to the end.

A reflection of itself is caught in the glass, but the shell sees nothing
but a pathetic creature,
A thought that was embedded long ago.

Disgusted by his own self-pity, there is a sudden desire to extinguish
his flame—to help rid the world of unwanted space.

Ruination and despair have won over his happiness.

Abandoned

Abandoned

Solitude: a horrible existence she has come to know. Each passing day the longing to hide increases—the desire to move forward wanes.

The blinds shut, she can no longer bear to look out to the light. Sadness, fits of rage, disoriented thoughts—all things she cannot explain. Struggling with reality, she is rapidly losing her sense of control.
As the episodes become more frequent,
the company she once held begins to diminish.

The young woman tries to rationalize her heartache and misfortune. Abandoned by her mind, her heart will not allow her to extinguish her feelings.

As the snow descends upon her aging home, she sits in the dark. Trying to grasp what is left of her world, wasted tears fill her lovely hazel eyes while a knife viciously cuts through her heart.

Pain, such pain!
Feelings of anger, resentment and sorrow wreak havoc on her.
That backstabbing heart! How dare it allow her to succumb to the heartache.

Her cries fill the silence in the desolate home.

The heart bleeds unmercifully for a life that has slipped away.

Dream

Anguish fills the holes in my severed heart, and with no remorse,
you stand and watch my destruction.

You vowed to love me through good times and bad. The child is
gone, and you are nowhere to be found.
Anger replaces contentment that was once found in my heart.

The memories crawl back in the depth of my mind.
I still hear the cheerful laughs, night after night, haunting my dreams.
Visions flood my dormant mind with thoughts of the family
we once were.
I try to escape, but I don't want to.

I yearn for my mind and body to find slumber, to forget the pain.
I yearn to have the light wash away the darkness.
I yearn for the unattainable.

Like your mother, you have abandoned me.
Your presence is longed for, but your soul has been taken. I yearn for
the lost child that cannot be found.

Kiss of Death

Kiss of Death

Darkness surrounds me; its only companion is the thick fog that is
slowly swallowing me whole.
I walk along the snow-covered path, and all I can hear is my dress as
it violently blows in the wind and the beat of my heart.
It starts to become louder, pounding in my chest as if it were
following the beat of a drum.

Da dum da dum
Da dum da dum
Da dum da dum

As I look around the mysterious forest, it appears as though this was
a once-beautiful area with great big open spaces that allowed you to
bask in the sunshine.
Beautiful stone benches that would have sparkled in the sun's light are
now crumbling and covered with moss and broken branches.
The once-vast area is encroached with trees that are overpowering and
unnatural looking. Ever so tall when you look upon them and
bunched together that you feel barricaded from everything else.
It was as if these eerie, dark-looking trees had chased the light away.

Da dum da dum
Da dum da dum
Da dum da dum

Pressure—that is all I remembering feeling,
from friends, family, and work.
It was just never good enough; I always felt out of place,
even in my own skin.

Now all those things seem like a distant memory that I no longer have to worry about.
As I tightly wrap my hand, a white candlestick to help break through this thick fog flashes go through my mind—tears, resentment, anger, a knife.

Da dum da dum
Da dum da dum
Da dum da dum

My heart feels faint, and I hear echoes of voices.
Looking down at my blood-stained hands
I realize what I have done.
A decision I cannot return from.

Da dum da dum
Da dum da dum
Da dum da dum

The remnants of myself burn before me.
With every stride I take, a layer of me sheds to the ground—
The girl I was,
the woman I am,
and the woman I would have been.

Da dum da dum
Da dum da dum
Da dum da dum

In the middle of this unnatural forest, it dawns on me why this voyage must be taken alone.
I blow out the candle and let the fog devour my body.

Aurora

Drained of all energy, Aurora lies in her fading garden upon a bed adorned with flowers. She is exposed and abandoned; a dark shadow creeps upon her slowly. Looking toward the heavy mist that had hovered over the forest, she sees its hand now stretching toward the once-vibrant garden. Aurora shivers, as she knows what is coming.

Breaking her deep gaze from the inevitable ruin, the lost girl turns her delicate body to greet the rising sun. A bold smile is discovered on her pale face. Embracing the sunlight, Aurora delicately rises to her feet. The warmth of the sun's golden rays is felt throughout her body, revitalizing her limbs.

The luscious, green grass cushions her steps, and Aurora glides toward the light, a surge of strength pulsing through her. The paleness begins to shy away, allowing the colour to come forward on her youthful face. Standing tall before the sun, her long red locks of hair flow behind her as she feels the last few remnants of the crisp autumn breeze before the arrival of winter.

Aurora tightly wraps her pearl white shawl to cover her bare shoulders. At one time, the shawl had shielded her from the pains of the world, but the cruelness became too much to bear, cutting its way through the cloth to her heart.

With a smile on her face, Aurora closes her eyes and reminisces of the times of joy she once felt, longing for the company of old to be around once more. Friendships she held so near and dear to her heart slowly drifted out of her life like a cool breeze. Childhood friends promising to be with her until her dying days were nowhere to be found when called upon.

Loves that greedily preyed upon her were taken by the night when their thirst was quenched. Bonds that were forged by blood were broken by their conditional love. A woman full of love, a shining beacon of hope, Aurora was passed around, leaving her heart destitute and her body drained. Lost in a world of hate and selfishness, her gift of light was put to the side like a worn-out Christmas gift.

Fearful of the solitude she now finds herself in, she lets her thoughts stray to the dark too often. The shadows befriend her and ease the pain since she cannot find solace elsewhere.

The further she retreats in her mind, the higher the walls become around her, shielding her radiance from all to see. Blocking the pain from the outside, she does not see how the pain she harbours is harming her.

Drops of light rain begin to fall upon her face and trickle down to the earth. Opening her eyes, Aurora looks up to see the clouds, darker and gathered together as if they are mounting an attack. Quickly, the blockade moves towards the sun, decimating the rays of light and covering the sky in darkness. Seeing this change, Aurora cautiously retreats to her fortress, stumbling as she feels something heavy at the pit of her stomach. Her face fills with sadness, for she knows what darkness is about to fall upon her.

A black plague she once stumbled across, unknowingly accepting the darkness for company—she did not realize it would eventually consume her. Remaining dormant for so long, it had lingered and waited for the right time to strike, now, no longer willing to be ignored. The presence has grown stronger with each passing day, slowly eating away at her soul.

Scared, Aurora concentrates hard on the remaining light, trying to give one last fight. Hearing a voice, she holds her place and listens for what she does not know. Her eyes quickly search the scene, but no one is to be seen. Hearing it again, she jumps; it was closer this time, much closer. Feeling a cold breath upon her neck, she frantically looks around. Still no one is there.

"Aurora," the shadow says in a raspy voice.

Looking up, all she can see is the dense fog beginning to encircle her garden. In a trembling voice, she speaks out to the emptiness. "Who's there?"

Out of fright, she does not dare to move a muscle, holding very still. Hearing only the mutterings of the hoarse voice, she listens with even more intent. Menacingly, the voice calls her name again, bringing a chill down her back.

Cautiously, she speaks out. "Stop hiding! I know something is out there."

"Why so sad, Aurora?" the voice asks sarcastically. "You, who are so bright and fair, lovelier than all those in the world—why are you alone and crying?"

Confused as to what is happening, she hesitantly speaks. "Why, stranger, do my affairs concern you?"

Mocking her pain, the shadow laughs at her. "Silly little girl, have all those you've encountered hurt you so much that you have lost all hope?"

Surprised by its harsh tone, Aurora does not know how to respond. She lifts her tearful eyes from the grass and looks up to see the black clouds eradicating the blue sky. The thick fog, spreading from the forest, begins to pick up speed and spills into her garden. Struggling to catch her breath, Aurora falls to her knees, the burden becoming too much to bear.

"All I have ever wanted is happiness. Is that too much to ask for?" she answers the mysterious voice. "At the end of each road I've taken I find only sorrow. I have been hurt too many times. I have continually pleaded with the world for peace, but like my need for happiness, my cries go unnoticed. The world has forsaken me."

Sobbing softly, she continues, "I've been sentenced to a life to watch others around me find the joy I desire, leaving me with the pains of not only my heart but the world."

Unable to continue, Aurora unleashes a wail of a cry, feeling the weight of the entire world pressing down upon her chest; she can no longer contain herself. Raising her fist, she curses the heavens for bestowing upon her this gift only for it to be wasted away. Crying in pain, she lies on her bed of flowers, her small hand covering her heart in hopes of protecting it.

"Why are you doing this to me?" she mutters through her cries.

The voice tauntingly replies to her, "The task of bringing sunlight to the world is your charge, so why is it your light is fading as others around you find the happiness you seek?" Enjoying her misery, the shadow unmercifully continues. "You are unable to love; you do not know how. That is why all have left you." The shadow hovers above her as she lies upon her flowers, her body growing colder. "Aurora, you were once happy, bright, and full of life. Now you are a mere vessel for fear and sadness to travel in. If you no longer continue to do your charge, the only solution will be to remove you."

Aurora tries to be strong as the shadow continues to snicker at her with a deep, cackling laugh.

"Stop it! That is not true; you will have no hold here. I will not let you. I will fight back!"

The clouds grow darker and the ground shakes as the voice leashes out a horrid laugh, echoing throughout her garden.

"Oh, you silly fool, do you not know when you have been defeated? You have nothing left in you anymore, no lingering feelings of love or kindness. No, they have been erased by jealously, sadness, and turmoil." Refusing to believe this, she sits up, shaking her head vigorously, trying to escape the deep and prominent, cold voice.

"No, it's not my fault," she continually repeats. "It's not me. It's not my fault! The world is too harsh."

Now larger, the shadow dismisses her words. "Aurora, if you still had sway, I would have been gone long ago. No, you kept me here. The time has come, Aurora, your light is fading, and you will part from this world."

A realization dawns upon Aurora—a realization that brings sadness to her face. She pleads with the darkness. "No, it was too much pain. I tried, but they drained me with their ignorance and refusal to learn and accept the world as it is. It's not my fault!" Screaming for help, she looks around her but sees only the intense fog encircling her garden, barricading her. Sobbing, she hangs her head low, her long, deep-red curls covering her face. She knows no one will answer her calls, for they all left long ago. Only the shadow remains to hear the echo of her trembling voice.

The mysterious voice roars a loud, hoarse laugh at her poor attempt at a defense.

"You are weak. Look at you—crying, hoping for some rescue from those who have already left you. Pathetic is what you are, a poor excuse of a creature."

"Please no, no more, just stop. It's not true, you speak lies," she manages to stammer out.

The shadow does not listen to reason and continues to break her down. "Look at you, lying there, weeping like a child. You are not a strong beacon of hope. That's why you are all alone."

Aurora stops, too drained and tired to continue any further. She stops arguing, stops caring; she gives up. Too much time and energy has been taken, leaving her emotionally crippled. No longer wanting to fight, the light allows the misery to overwhelm her.

The thick mist breaks the last barrier and crosses the threshold of the garden. It spreads itself around her, preparing to devour her.

Hearing the words of hate loud and clear now, she releases the tears held back for so many years. Her emerald green eyes overflow, and the tears begin to trickle down her cold, pale face.

In a low, eerie voice, the shadow of hate finishes the attack. "Lonely Aurora, no one around to care for you. All but I have left you."

She lays her broken body down upon her bed of flowers; her red locks spill upon the grass; her arms rest by her side; her smile vanishes. She bore all those harsh, lonely years on her own, more people mocking her than loving her. Everything piles upon her like a ton of bricks, all the hate, ignorance, and sadness weighing her down.

The world is changing around her; she no longer feels there is a place for her. The cold raindrops pour down her emotionless face, her entire body now cold and wet. Shivering, she gazes upon the withering garden and the heavens, trying to catch a glimpse of a ray of sunshine to save her. Her green eyes take their last look upon her decaying world, and as they close, she sees not a ray of light, but black hawks circling around the garden, waiting to feast upon her lifeless body.

With her last breath, she whispers ever so gently, "I tried."

The frail hand that once lay upon her beating heart falls to the ground, resting upon the dead flowers.

Love's Ghost

Love's Ghost

Sitting here thinking of you is all I seem to do.
A life that once had meaning is consumed with wasted thoughts of you.
Relentlessly pursuing me, accidental meetings and phone calls—anything that could bring us together.
I finally relented and let you in, unaware that I had sealed my own fate.

Flowers, gifts, all tokens of your love—you gave me everything but were never able to give me the one thing I wanted: your heart.
No, for it belonged to someone else.
The man I have come to love has now become the treasure I can never have.
Yet I still desire you, knowing you share another's bed.

I want to hate you, to purge all memories of your sweet, intoxicating smell, but my sentimental heart is compelled to long for you.

The ghosts of love will dance upon my grave and ridicule my pain.
In vain, I chase after you as the moon follows the sun.
Desperately trying to win something back that was never truly mine to begin with.

Emptiness

Emptiness

Hiding from prying eyes, he dwells in the corner, angry at how they changed him.
All of them having turning their backs on him long ago.

They cackle as they mock his pain.
He takes another sip to wash it away.
The emptiness remains.

Sucked into a war that was never his to begin with, he is left with memories that have "glory" and bring horror.

Alone, he drinks his sorrows away, hoping the heartache will be vanquished.
He tries to drown out the whistles and cries of joy from the vultures around him. The shadows start to play tricks; he sees things that are not there.

They cackle as they mock his pain.
He takes another sip to wash it away.
The emptiness remains.

The coldness of the world has broken his once-carefree heart.
No longer can he climb the ladder of racing rats,
Kicked down and spat upon one too many times.

They cackle as they mock his pain.
He takes another sip to wash it away.
The emptiness remains.

Shadows

With glowing hearts, we see thee rise.
With an open heart, he sees corruption win.
We stand on guard for thee—he is left limbless, to keep our land glorious and free.

They cackle as they mock his pain.
He takes another sip to wash it away.
The emptiness remains.

In the cold, he walks with his head down, hiding in winter's darkness.
Waiting for the day his meaningless life will end.
Broken and alone, he mourns his own heartache.

They cackle as they mock his pain.
He takes another sip to wash it away.
The emptiness remains.

Sorrow

Sorrow

Bewitched by the magic of love, I have strayed.
Whispers of sweet nothing, gentle strokes caressing
my face—actions that lured me into a vulnerable state.

I used to look in the mirror and see a strong,
determined woman.

Now I only see a broken girl.
Promises were broken as quickly
as they were made.
Hypnotized by his words,
I did not care. I became
lost in his world of
darkness with
no way out.
Soon the words of love
turned into hate.
Like bullets, each one
pierced my body, causing it
pain. The wounds are too deep.
All have left; tired of the same
story or bullied away, there is
no one to be found.
I can no longer see the light at the end of
the tunnel; darkness has swept in and has
left me in the winter's cold embrace.

One Wish

One Wish

Alone and depressed, I sit at the head of the table in my empty home.
I no longer know any other existence in the world but sadness.
Names and faces of old call out to me, and I crave the days that were filled with laughter and joy.

I can still feel the touch of her warm hand upon mine.
I can hear the laughs of my friends as we would entertain.
Opening my weary eyes, I now only see my grey, cold house with its crumbling roof, loose cupboards, and creaky floors.
Age has claimed my home, like it did her health.

I suffer through the long, cold winters with no relief.
Selfishly, the season remains, stealing the summer's light, leaving the young wild flowers to perish in the dark.
Loneliness fills my life.

Today marks another year where I am forced to be alone.
A day that was celebrated with joy I now look upon as a curse.
I can still hear her say, "A candle blown is a wish gained." Looking at the crumbling cake before me, I blow out the candle and wish for the bittersweet end.

Longing for the time when it was carefree, I wish time had stayed still so I could be as pure and innocent as a child until the end of my days.

Lake of Shadows

Lake of Shadows

Rubbing her muddy hands together, she looks away from her gardening and out past the hills, seeing the glistening lake. The young woman feels the water calling to her, but voices from the past creep in her head, saying no: stories told to her as a child, people who went missing after they ventured towards the lake. Never can she go near it, her father constantly told her. *Mischievous*, that is the word she remembers her father calling it. As a child, she obeys, but as a woman, she is bold and stubborn, ready to prove anyone wrong.

Her curiosity gets the better of her.

Only to clean her hands, she thought, no harm could come from that. She ponders, dropping the flower stems from her hands.

Submerged in the bewitching lake she slowly makes her way to the surface. Allowing her body to sway in the unusually warm waters, she gracefully floats in a lake of lost hopes and dreams. Her small delicate hand floats above her head, shielding her eyes as a stream of pale light crosses over her. Intrigued, she begins to swim toward it, but the water will not allow it. The harder she tries to move toward the light the further she is submerged.

She feels her body being weighed down by her failures and limitations. Her bright eyes search the water to find something to help pull her up. She sees nothing but a vast lake with no beginning or end. Now regretting her decision, she realizes her stubbornness has led her astray.

Suddenly the water begins to toss and turn, and the waves become rougher. Her fragile body is thrown from side to side; frantically she tries to fight against the great tide. Drowning, she desperately tries to reach a firm grip but finds nothing. The lake fights her every stroke, selfishly trying to add to its collection of lost souls.

Long ago, their bodies were all found, washed up on shore for the living to lament their unknown existence. Their once-vibrant spirits, now claimed by the vast blue lake, dwell within, haunting the mysterious girl.

Swirling around her, they raise their ghost-like hands to her scared face. They will not allow her to escape. They beckon her to join them, another watery grave to add to the lake of sorrow.

The current violently heaves her body, twisting and tormenting her like a rag doll. She fights back with all her might, trying to gasp for air. The waves hurl her back to the bosom of the lake. The lost souls tug at her long, silky hair and tear at her body until she takes her last breath.

She sees nothing but darkness, and the lake swallows her whole.

Lake of Shadows

Her eyes wide-open but empty, her body floats on the calm surface.

There, the living look upon the contoured body and mourn for the unknown soul.

They weep for her, another victim of the lake. Eventually moving along with their lives. Yet, she remains among the company of the dead, with her lost dreams and aspirations. Patiently they wait, ready to claim their next victim.

Starlight

Starlight

Like a diamond, I used to shine bright above the sky.
My light stolen, only a black hole remains.

A world I once had no fear of has slowly eaten me alive.
Sheltered, I did not see friend from foe.
Naive, I could not see his true light.
Taken is my innocence.

Unable to move forward, I dwell on the unfortunate.
Bitter are my thoughts.
Forced to see the horror in the world, I am unable to see the light.

Shed no tears for me; I am already dead.
What you see before you is just a shadow waiting to diminish.

The Last Waltz

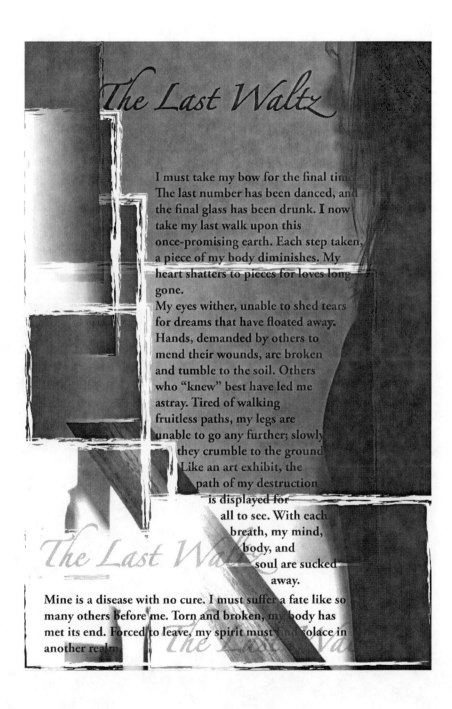

The Last Waltz

I must take my bow for the final time.
The last number has been danced, and
the final glass has been drunk. I now
take my last walk upon this
once-promising earth. Each step taken,
a piece of my body diminishes. My
heart shatters to pieces for loves long
gone.
My eyes wither, unable to shed tears
for dreams that have floated away.
Hands, demanded by others to
mend their wounds, are broken
and tumble to the soil. Others
who "knew" best have led me
astray. Tired of walking
fruitless paths, my legs are
unable to go any further; slowly
they crumble to the ground.
Like an art exhibit, the
path of my destruction
is displayed for
all to see. With each
breath, my mind,
body, and
soul are sucked
away.

Mine is a disease with no cure. I must suffer a fate like so
many others before me. Torn and broken, my body has
met its end. Forced to leave, my spirit must find solace in
another realm.

Memory

Memory

Gentle snowflakes descend upon my face.
Neither a sound to be heard nor a creature to be seen.
I have left all in search of solitude.

Slowly I feel my sanity slipping away.
I am unable to remember the littlest tasks; names that were as familiar as my own seem so distant.

I walk away, not allowing myself to be a burden onto others.
I shall get lost in the open space of the world along with my memories.

On the horizon, there is a speck of sunshine.
I am unable to smile at the light. My eyes shed tears for happiness long gone, for I am unable to remember.

Fading

Fading

Our love flourished as a flower blooms and faded as quickly as a flower wilts.
Before our beauty could be appreciated, you tore my heart out without a second thought.

Young and foolish, I did not know how to love you the way you wanted to be love.
Your absence became longer, leaving our bed cold.
Sneakily you hid from me, the shadows concealing your true light.

Secret phone calls,
Secret rendezvous—
It was always a friend in need.

Foolish was I to believe the friend did not also need a bed to lie in.
All that is left is my heart to feel the effects of her poisonous thorns.

Lost

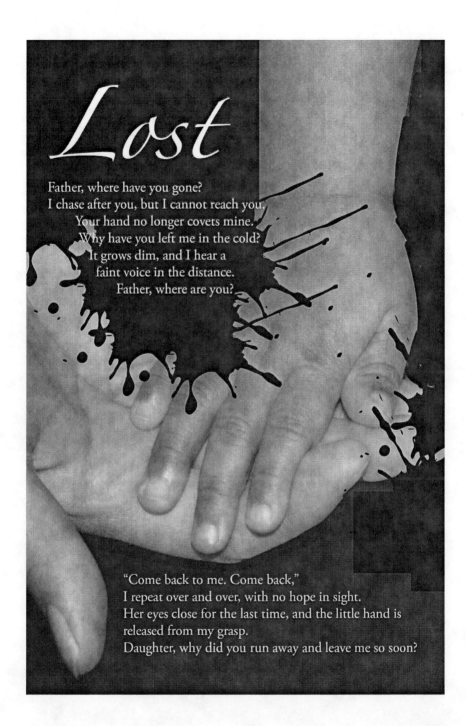

Lost

Father, where have you gone?
I chase after you, but I cannot reach you.
    Your hand no longer covets mine.
      Why have you left me in the cold?
        It grows dim, and I hear a
          faint voice in the distance.
            Father, where are you?

"Come back to me. Come back,"
I repeat over and over, with no hope in sight.
Her eyes close for the last time, and the little hand is
released from my grasp.
Daughter, why did you run away and leave me so soon?

Section II

Drops of rain fall upon my face, cleansing the wounds of my past. Spring shall revitalize the earth and my soul.

Angel

Angel

I willed our bond to die so I could breathe again.
I am turning my back on your troubles and needs
as you have turned away from me.

I will forget the love and support unselfishly bestowed
upon me as you have chosen to erase the memory of me.

Sheltered no longer by your love, each step I have taken is to move
away from home.

I break away not so I can hurt you, but in order to live a life I want,
with no constraints or judgments.

I break away to no longer be under your mothering hand.

A Cry for Help

A Cry for Help

Death has taken you, and I remain behind, yearning for it.
Day turns to night, night turns to day, and all that is constant is this unbearable pain I feel within me.

The light in my world has disappeared. All that I am left with is the light of the stars, and even they seem to mock my pain. They sparkle bright in the vast sky, only to dim as I approach.

I yearn for the light once again—to feel the warmth upon my skin, to have your strong arms hold me again. Memories of you are slowly slipping away; dark thoughts are sneaking in, taking control.
I want to remember the days that were once filled with happiness, but all I seem to remember is flashes of sadness whenever I think of you.

There was a loud noise. I turned back and saw you hold on to your stomach in a pool of blood. I heard the roar of the sirens, the hysteria of the crowd, and you calling out to me. Cradled in my arms, all you could utter out was "Hold me tight. I'm scared." With that, your eyes were lifeless, and my heart was crushed.

O sun, please return!
Bring back the light the night has blocked.

Arise from your slumber and shine your golden rays.
Help me find the strength to walk in your light again.

Become a beacon to the one who has strayed.

Gone Too Soon

Gone Too Soon

He sits in a dark corner clinging to the wall, like a scared cat in a dark alley; wishing she would come back. He remembers the day when she was taken away.

A somber crowd gathers in the kitchen and hovers around the phone. When the conversation ends, an older man has his head down. Scrambling for words, the man does not know what to say.

The only words the boy can remember are "I have some bad news." It plays in his head like a broken record. At that moment, it becomes clear what happened.

The boy watches as his father breaks down and sheds unmerciful tears for his lost mother.

Not knowing what to do with himself, the boy wanders upstairs and sits against the wall in a room. Unsure if he should cry, the child reminisces of stories told to him, not having his own first accounts, for he had never met her. Wishing he could have seen her, he is prepared to give his soul to the devil himself. He needed to know why this strong woman mesmerized everyone.

At times, he thinks if they had met, he would not have been captivated by her charms. He hates to think that, so in the end he believes it was best they never did.

Others tell him that it was her time and that "everyone has to go at some point."

He looks at her photograph—and though she was old, he thinks to himself she is gone too soon.

Regrets

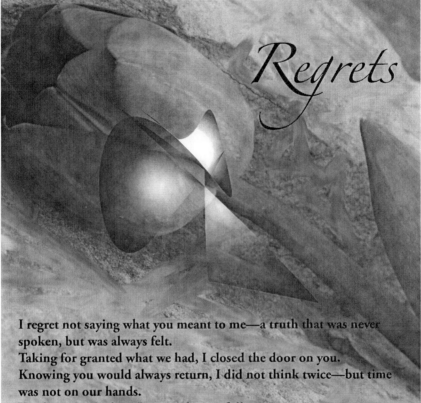

Regrets

I regret not saying what you meant to me—a truth that was never spoken, but was always felt.
Taking for granted what we had, I closed the door on you.
Knowing you would always return, I did not think twice—but time was not on our hands.
You have gone where I can no longer follow.
We were on borrowed time and the fates reclaimed their prize.
Unknowingly you took your last drive and were snatched at your prime. How many years must I walk upon this earth alone?

There were so many actions that cannot be undone,
So many things unsaid.
So many regrets now remain that I shall always carry, but with the bad there is the good.
With a heavy heart and once-happy memories, I shall cherish every moment we shared.

Lady in Blue

Lady in Blue

Beaming, she stands in the middle of the candlelit ballroom in her deep blue silk gown. Her bubbly spirit captivates bystanders as she gaily throws her head back, laughing. Warmth, the sound of music, and laughter fill the bustling room.

Joyous is the occasion, but there is something in the air this night. She can feel it. She cannot put her finger on it, but she knows it is not like any other night.

Enchanted by the sound of the piano, the lady in blue glides arm in arm with a charming man and dances the night away. Her smile is bold and delightful, fooling all those who gaze upon her—an illusion she not only has for them, but also for herself.

Across the ballroom, he watches her over the frolicking crowd, wondering if she still remembers the time they shared. Befriending the shadows, he lurks along the walls with his eyes intently on her, catching only glimpses of her black, shiny hair as the dancers weave through each other like an intricate ballet. Yearning to see her angelic face again, he risks a bit more light and steps forward, using the passing bodies as shields. A clearing opens, and he is able to see her smile light up the room. He instantly regrets the time that was lost.

Suddenly, a gust of wind blows through the stained glass doors, bringing in the crisp leaves. Traveling throughout the room, the colourful foliage makes its descent, circling the blue-dressed beauty and falling gently onto the ground. Turning her head toward the doors that lead to the gardens, she catches a glance of a man staring at her. Before she can react, he quickly retreats to the shadows and loses himself among the crowd, which scrambles to find shelter from the autumn winds.

Distracted by the mystery man, she loses her train of thought. Unaware of why she cares, she only knows that she does. Leaning closer to the man she is dancing with, she softly speaks. "I'm going to get some fresh air." He looks upon her face and solemnly nods.

Making her way through the intoxicated crowd, she opens up the French doors to be embraced by a gentle cool breeze. Gazing at the stars, she strolls towards the edge of the stone veranda, finally beginning to feel her body cool down. Closing her eyes as she runs her fingers through her long, silky hair, she starts humming to the melody playing inside. Standing contently with a smile on her face, she feels as though something is amiss. Sadly, she is not aware that the problem lies with her. The world sees only a strong person, but there is a hole within her that she conceals. Cruelly ripped away, her heart finds the winter too soon and is unable to uncover the shining sun. The emptiness soon becomes filled with the taste of alcohol, which she finds herself drowning in.

Turning to face the vintage ballroom, she looks upon the crowd and feels contempt for them. She begins to hate all of them for their happiness and joy and herself for allowing them to engage her in it. The sorrow becoming too much for her, she quickly drinks out of her glass to quench the ache. Each sip she takes brings her the comfort she is yearning for.

The black-haired beauty has become empty inside, clinging to lost memories while resenting any happiness that does come her way. She has come to believe that she does not deserve any happiness. Saddened, she makes her way inside again, her sights set on the bar.

Outside, he stands on the veranda, taking in the brisk breeze as he watches her smile in the middle of the crowd. Desiring only to hold her again, all he can do is find cover in the shadows—missing the way she would laugh at his jokes even when they were not funny, remembering the way he would run his hand down her smooth back when she lay beside him at night. He counted the years until he could see her again. Now that day is upon him, he does not know what to do. He thinks to himself how beautiful she looks with her long hair, black as the night, her grey eyes sparkling like stars, and her sleeveless gown, the shade of the deep blue sea and cut low so he can see her entire back. He yearns for her and cannot wait to have her in his arms again.

Now on her third drink, she feels as though she is being watched again. Turning her body, she sees a tall figure standing where she was a little while ago, near the garden doors. She notices that it is the same man from before. She can barely make him out; only the light of the moon illuminates him for her eyes to see. Though she can only see his shadow, she feels as if she knows who he is. Hearing her name called to join the party, she ignores the summons and is compelled to walk over to the man in the black suit.

With every step she takes, the people begin to fade away. Eventually, all that is left is a deserted ballroom with remnants of life at one point in time. Making her way back to the terrace, she finds a spot and stands silently in the still of the night. Looking out over the gardens, she waits for this mystifying man to reappear. She hears the sound of tapping and is intrigued. The sound lures her, and she finds herself walking toward the end of the veranda, where she finds the man she is seeking.

Holding her place and not knowing what else to do, she lingers so he will turn around and face her. It annoys her that he refuses to pay attention to her; instead, he looks down at his watch impatiently, as if he is waiting for someone. For some reason, it appears to her that time is quickly running out for him.

Bored with the lack of interaction, she takes another sip of her wine, and as she does, he slowly lifts his head and turns around to face her. A look of utter shock fills her face, and the glass shatters on the floor. Confused and unsure of what to do, she tries to collect her thoughts in those few seconds she has, for he runs off toward the gardens. With her mind a complete blank, the only certain thing for her to do is to follow him—or take the risk of losing him again.

She is not sure how this is possible, for she was told he had left and was never returning. Pushing her questions aside, she focuses only on following him. She needs answers, and she wants them now.

As she runs through the gardens, memories flash through her mind repeatedly. She remembers a time when she was walking down her street to get the mail. Turning the corner, she saw him walking his dog—well, more like the other way around. He was chasing him, trying to grab hold of the leash. She stood there laughing at the sight. He caught her eye; quickly, she turned around, breaking the intent glance.

Looking back at the memory now, she realizes that she is looking into the eyes of the man who will forever change her life—the one person worth living for, something she realizes only after they part ways.

This man is not just her friend or first love, but he is her soul mate. He is the one who protects her from all of the darkness. He is not afraid to tell her when she is wrong and still loves her unconditionally. When he left her, there was no one else to hold off the darkness, and soon after it overwhelmed her.

Panting, she can feel how hot her cheeks have become. Frantically searching for a glimpse of him, she tries listening for his footsteps, but all she can hear is the shuffling of the shrubs she is running through. The only thing there to guide her through the maze of gardens is the light of the moon. Her thoughts still wild and random, her pace hastens.

Her mind backtracks, and the only constant thought she has is how she always knew their paths would unfailingly cross each other's. The lady in blue is right: their paths did always cross, and the last time they did meet, it had forever changed her.

It was a very cold winter evening; making her way through a large and somber crowd, she waited until they could be together. Staggering into one of the empty rooms and trying to get away from the crowd, she waited alone and in peace.

She is taken aback when she finds that the room she entered was the room he was already in. Hesitant, she crept up to him; he was asleep, dressed in a black suit with his hands folded on his stomach. The cold winter draft swept in as she reached out for his cold hand and felt a chill go down her back.

Softly, she whispered into his ear so as not to startle him from his slumber. "Wake up. Please wake up. I have something to tell you." He ignored her gentle voice.

Repeatedly, she called out to him and pleaded for him to acknowledge her. He did not; instead, he persisted in lying there in silence. Angered, she stood back, looking hard at his face. "Fine, then, be that way!" she yelled as she stomped out of the room in tears, filled with hate. In that cold, dark room, her love for him was left behind, and she took the resentment and bitterness away with her. She stayed angry with him for a long time, not willing to forgive him. While the man in black cherished the love, she left in the room with him. He did not allow himself to forget and wished he were able to wake up to reassure her.

The memories stirred within her, she is very eager to see him again. She begins to ponder aloud the things that she will say to him. Despite all the curse words that are thought of, none of them are used when the moment comes.

Continuing to scramble through the garden, having run out of breath long ago, she forces herself to go on.

Pausing at the edge of a small wooden bridge over a brook, she takes in deep, long breaths. She searches her surroundings and sees a path that leads into another garden, full of lilies. The lady in blue tries to recollect her thoughts and focus.

Enclosed by the beauty of the grounds, she surveys the area to see which path he may have taken. A bit lost and confused, the lady begins to question herself, not sure if she is imagining the whole thing. The blue-dressed beauty starts to think she has made a mistake. It did happen before; it was always a case of mistaken identity.

Turning around to make her way back up to the main house, she pauses as she hears a faint sound. Someone is whistling. Led by the mysterious sound, she follows a series of windings that lead her to a small, black iron gate. This garden seems different to her compared to the others; it seems to have isolated itself from the rest of the gardens. Rather than being encircled by vibrant green hedges, there is a tall stone wall that is barricaded itself: you would not be able to tell there was even a wall there unless you ran right into it, for it is covered in ivy from top to bottom.

She pushes open the creaky gate with her shaky hand, and her foot crosses over the threshold. A narrow stone path lies before her and leads the lady through, past the overbearing trees with lilies growing all around them. The space is tight; her silk dress keeps snagging on the bushes.

The space soon opens up to the middle of the garden, where a white gazebo covered in lights stands high in the center of the open ground. The trees are kept at a distance but still encircle the gazebo. All that grows near it are the white lilies that are spread throughout the garden.

He stands in the center of the gazebo with his back facing her, waiting. Cautiously, she walks toward him, pausing at the foot of the steps, frightened he may run away again.

The lady in blue waits a few moments before breaking the eerie silence, for she is unsure what will happen. Gently uttering his name, she catches his attention, and he ceases to look at his watch. Slowly, he turns around to face the one he has abandoned. She climbs the steps draped in colourful petals and stops right in front of him, hesitant to have any further contact for fear of him vanishing at the mere touch of her hand.

In a tender voice, he speaks to her. "You're late. I've been waiting for you."

Her heart begins to pound as she stares into his brown eyes, and she cannot help but notice there is something different. Something is absent; the spark that was once there is gone.

Lifting her trembling hand from her side, she reaches for his cheek but hesitates out of fear. Taking her retreating hand, he ever so gently places it upon his cheek for her. As she softly strokes his cool cheek, he speaks to her.

"I am real, and I won't be leaving you this time."

Opening her mouth to say something, any of the things that ran through her mind, she is at a complete loss for words. All that she says is "I miss you."

At that moment, he embraces her, softly kissing her lips with no intention of letting her go.

While they enjoy the warmth of each other's bodies, a gust of wind sweeps over them, carrying a gathering of petals that gently descends upon them. He removes his jacket and places it around her bare shoulders, embracing her ever more closely.

"How is this possible?" the lady in blue asks. "You're not supposed to be here."

"Why? Would you rather me leave?" he responds.

"No, I never wanted you to leave me in the first place, but you're supposed to be . . ."

Choking up as the words try to come out, she looks upon his face with watery eyes, trying to muster the courage to speak again.

"You can't be here, because you're dead—aren't you?"

Looking into her grey eyes while stroking her luscious hair, he responds, "I am."

Satisfied with the answer, she understands what has happened and places her head upon his chest, enjoying the fact that she is able even to touch him—let alone speak to him—again. No longer does she care about the reasons why or what will happen. It does not matter, for she is reunited with the man in black; the soul is complete once again.

There, under the moon's light, they stand together in each other's arms, not needing nor wanting anything else, for they have found each other again. No longer in the world of the living, they remain forever in the world of the unknown, forever bound by each other's love.

Letting Go

Letting Go

The skies are black, and the future is blank.
There is no sound or movement I can make.
A body that was once robust is now lifeless.

Never forget the memories shared.
Always remember the wisdom bestowed.
Do not dwell on the moments I will not be there to share.
I am only a thought away.

Bring forth the mourners;
Adorn me in my finest;
Praise my success;
Forgive my mistakes.

Set my body afire and release my soul.
Save your remorse, for death has taken me home.

Falling

I keep falling,
    falling,
    falling.
I found you as my outlet;
you saw me as your exit.
I keep falling,
    falling,
    falling.
I turned to you for love and support;
you turned your fist on me.
I keep falling,
    falling,
    falling.
No longer can I live in fear.
Dragging my courage with me, I walk out the door, leaving the stench of alcohol.
I keep falling,
    falling,
    falling.
There is no return.
No longer will I fear your fists, like the stories told to me about monsters in my closet, I will outgrow the fear.
I keep falling,
    falling,
    falling.
When will I reach the earth?
When will I soar again?

Spring Fling

Spring Fling

Another night has passed, and the hole remains.
It seals itself as darkness fills the skies, and tears open as I greet the rising sun.
Pain ravishes my body as I remember your sweet breath upon my neck.

The memories we have shared are suffocating me. I feel the walls closing in.

"Routine" and "repetitive" are the words you threw at me. "I have outgrown us," you sweetly said as you walked out the door.
Life is cruel to have my love bestow their heart upon me, only to be the very one to crush my own.

With every barrier that I face, I yearn to self-destruct, but with each stumble, I will grow stronger. Soon I will be released from this spell.

The April showers will renew the earth and wash away the dirt and revitalize the life within me.

Thief in the Night

Theif in the Night

Why do you cry in the night?
Who has taken the light from your eyes?
What monster has taken flight with your jewel?

A thief in the night has left you hurt and scared.
Seduced by his words, you did not see his true light.
The fire within you no longer burns as bright.

Alone and scared, you now hide in the night.
What words were used to break you?
What foot stomped on your spirit?

Did the thief take pleasure in your plight?
Did a smile light his face when he left you?
The thief in the night underestimated your spirit.

Why do you still cry in the night?
Come out into the light.
Burn bright once again.

Fall from Grace

Fall from Grace

Warm blood trickles down my hands,
Sliced from the jagged-edged mountain you built.
I continue to climb each layer that you impose.
Your love for me was the reason, or so you said.

My legs tremble beneath me. My body begins to stumble.
But I hold on; I hold on to us.

Reaching the top, I see your beautiful face smiling down on me.
My hand reaches out to you.
Your eyes turn cold, the smile fades, and you let go.

No balance, I slip.
With outstretched arms, I tumble to the earth.
My body becomes light as a feather,
Flowing easily with the wind.

The further I fall, the less pain I feel.
My judgment is no longer cloudy.
I can see you for who you really are.

I will survive this fall.

Destiny

Destiny

The world lies on one side of the universe, and on the other there is you. Terror fills this vast space in which we must endure in order to be reunited. Long ago, our destiny was written in tears. It was a love so great that it brought envy to those who watched.

The fates, cold and unfeeling, were cruel to us; they deemed us unworthy of their kindness. Their jealously soon turned to malice, wanting to part us.

They struck their wrath upon us, separating us into two. Yet we defied their hatred, and our love grew stronger. We were made for each other, and it was only in body that we were now parted.
Outraged at our defiance, the agents of destiny sought our destruction. They would not allow us to be in this world together. Manipulatively, spinning our thread of life at their will and cut upon our golden line too soon.

Our parting brought such sorrow that the stars, unable to shine, covered the sky with their tears, gracefully falling upon the earth.
Two souls with a love so pure were now condemned to spend eternity searching for each other.

I wait in the vast space of the universe for your return.

Perseverance

Perseverance

The wound is deep, the dagger still piercing the skin. The chains of society weigh down on me. The ache cuts through all of my dreams and hopes.
The warm blood trickles down, washing away all of my aspirations.

The future is blank. I look ahead, and I see no light, no happiness. Where is my miracle?

I close my eyes and picture a world with no pain. A smile is found upon my face—I have the power.

I will take on what lies ahead, and I will be strong.
I will not be confined.
I will be true to myself.

I stretch my arm out as far as it will allow as I unwind the heavy bonds around my body. Society's judgment and jealousy, its misconceptions, are making it difficult to move. The bonds tear through my skin, burning as I pull upon each one. I find the restraint becoming stronger with each fallen chain.

My bleeding body throbs, but I do not relent. I will fight this losing battle. My struggle will help someone else's victory.

A Glimpse of Light

A Glimpse of Light

Darkness spreads throughout the sky, and with it comes a bitter cold.
Frost begins to settle upon the earth.
A look of fear appears on the child's face.

They all stand and watch as the hand of darkness spreads throughout their world, bringing ruin and devastation. Not a single body stirred to prevent it; no, rather, they joined in the destruction of their own existence. One by one, they all begin to fall.

Abandoned, the lonely child shivers in the cold. Giving up all hope, he roams the bare land.

Suddenly, streams of light pierce the grey clouds, falling upon the castaway. Rays of sunshine scoop up the child from the darkness. Bringing salvation, the radiant sun leads the way home.

Roots

Like a tree's, her roots are deep in the earth.
As the tree stands tall for all to see, so does she.
Every force of nature can throw its wrath upon her:

Lightning can bear down leaving behind scars,
but can never strike her down.
Gusts of wind can ravage her but will never be
able to destroy her beauty. Hail can come down
in torrents, but in time, the spirit mends.

Through all perils, the roots are resilient, leaving
her strong.Not allowing herself to sway to unknown
darkness, she continually bestows her tender heart to
those around her.

Taking on every challenge that comes her way she will
face it with her head held high.

It is a sight to be seen through all the ages.

A Point in Time

A Point in Time

I am loved, but I am judged.
I am given freedom, but when I grow, I am stopped.
When I shine, I am shunned for my brightness.

For years, a glass box has been my home; there, I am admired by all but ignored for my capabilities.
Like the strings on a harp, I am plucked at the will of my captor,
Forced to hit notes I do not wish to play.

My song is slowly silencing.

Patiently I wait; I see a crack in the glass.
Patiently I wait; my body is getting restless.
Patiently I wait; my jailer is distracted.
My time is here.

With clenched fists, I break my cage, shattering the glass house.
Free of all bonds and limitations, I leave behind my jailer.
I walk out to the world a new person beginning a new journey.
I face a long, treacherous walk into the unknown—
But I am free to live.

Farewell

Farewell

An embrace full of warmth has now turned cold.
The soft touch of a kiss left bitterness upon my lips—
A fond farewell to the one I loved.

I turn away with sadness in my heart, but my head held high.
I leave the past behind in the dust and look toward a new dawn.

Acknowledgments

This book has been in the making for a long time now. I always wanted to be a writer, and if it were not for my family and friends, that dream would have died a long time ago. Had it not been for their kind words and encouragement, I do not think I would have ever been able to follow through. There are a few people in particular whom I would like to thank.

The first person I would have to acknowledge is my sister. Thank you, Sunny, your blind faith in me and your refusal to allow me to quit have made me see this to the end.

Misha, thank you for your genuine happiness for me and your willingness to help me on this journey. Jasmine, thank you for all of your kind words and support. Kate, thanks for being honest about my work and forcing me to do better.

Sand and Nestor, thanks for helping me with my vision of text and image come to life. Sand you have done a lovely job with the book cover.

Heidi, thank you for being you and providing the inspiration that allowed me to continue writing this book. Bal and Sue, I want to thank you for everything you both have done for me.

Finally, I would like to thank my husband, Dennis. You gave me strength when I could not find it. The love, support and courage you continually show me, means everything to me.

I want to thank my entire family and all of my friends for your love and encouragement. To the great staff at iUniverse thank for your guidance and patience. With everyone's help, I was able to turn one of my dreams into a reality, and I will be forever grateful.

CPSIA information can be obtained at www.ICGtesting.com
Printed in the USA
LVOW131128280313

326378LV00001B/2/P